Enjoy meeting Brinkley

Berner Bless,

Laura and

THINK

BRINK

The Tails of Brinkley the Berner

Art director: Laura Leah Johnson
Design and production: Bethany Argisle, Argisle Enterprises, Inc., and Albert Howell, Meta4 Productions.

Library of Congress Cataloging-in-Publication Data.

Johnson, Laura Leah, 1947 –
The Tails of Brinkley the Berner / Laura Leah Johnson; illustrated by Jen-Ann Kirchmeier.
Summary: A heart-warming true story of the loving friendship between two very special Bernese Mountain dogs.

ISBN 978-0-9793288-0-0 (Hard cover)

1. Children 2. Family 3. Animals
I. Kirchmeier, Jen-Ann, ill. II. The Tails of Brinkley the Berner

Laura Leah Johnson / Brinkley Books, Inc.™
PO Box 1753, Healdsburg, CA 95448

Printed in Singapore
10 9 8 7 6 5 4 3 2 1

Photographs courtesy of JC Meadows Photography

The Tails of Brinkley the Berner

The Beginning

By Laura Leah Johnson

Brinkley Books, Inc.
www.brinkleybooks.com

In loving memory of
my Mother.
May this book find its way
to you in heaven.

ABOUT BRINKLEY I am a 93-pound Bernese Mountain dog and my name is Brinkley. My nickname is Binkie. Bernese Mountain dogs come from Switzerland and sometimes they are called Berners. It is important for me to be kind to others, people and dogs, faithful and loving to my Momma and Daddy, and treasure my friend-ships. This is a true story of the friendship that I treasure most. This story is about my best friend, Luca James, and me.

ABOUT LUCA My name is Luca James and I am a three and a half year old Bernese Mountain dog. My birthday is Valentine's Day and that is why I have a big heart filled with so much love. Binkie and I have taught each other so many things. He came into my life when he was three months old. His Momma and Daddy were go-ing on vacation and he needed a babysitter. My Momma and Auntie own "Walkies" (a profession-al pet care company). We came to his house and from the first time we met, we knew we would be friends forever. Binkie is a very special friend.

My real name is Brinkley but my Momma has called me Binkie since I was a baby boy puppy. I am a nine month old Bernese Mountain dog.

This is a true story about my best friend, Luca James, and me. Luca is a Bernese Mountain dog just like me.

I live in the country with my Momma and Daddy. We board two horses, Chrissy and Snoopy, two piggies, Fred and Wilma, and Bodacious, a black angus steer, and lots of jackrabbits are running all around. Our town is very small and has a park in the center where dogs sometimes meet and visit.

When I first met Luca, he came running into
the kitchen and jumped over my baby gate.

Wow, I thought. He was so big and strong.
He was a lot bigger than me. I took one look at
him and knew we would be friends forever.

Luca's Momma would bring him over to take care of me. He taught me so many things. I learned to play with my friend and share my toys. He told me it is important to be very kind to your friends and always share what you have. Luca is very gentle with me when we play. We share my water bowl and treats. We share everything, because that is what best friends do.

After we play a lot, we have a snack. Then it is time to rest. I always lay close to my friend. While we are resting, we cross paws. Sometimes I think quiet time is the best time so we can just snuggle and be together.

Luca told me about a special place we would go when I got bigger – the dog park. He said there are lots of trees and small hills to run around and other dogs to play with. When you get thirsty, there are plenty of water bowls to drink from.

The time had finally come when I was old enough to go to the dog park. I did not see Luca at first, but then he came running towards me. He had lots of friends with him. Some looked just like us and some didn't. Some had short tails, some had long tails. Some had big ears, some had little ears. Some had all different colored fur, and some had only one color. Some had short fur, some had long fur. Some just had so much fur that was all you could see!

Luca introduced me to all the dogs. I was nervous but Luca stayed with
me and told me to play just like he taught me. We all took off running
up the hill and down. Sometimes we would wrestle and tumble in the
grass. Luca said he was very proud of his little buddy. We had such fun!
Before I knew it, it was time to go home. Boy, do I love the park!

Winter was coming and I was getting bigger. It rains a lot where we live. Since we could not go to the park, Luca and I play inside.

We spend hours just running and playing with my toys. Luca still loves to play "keep away." Since I was getting bigger, sometimes I would get the toy and run. Then we would lie on the living room floor and toss and tumble. Luca would tickle me and I would laugh and laugh. Sometimes I would tickle him back.

Luca told me Christmas was coming and to make a list of toys and treats I wanted. Luca said we would go with our parents to meet Santa and to bring my list. Momma was busy decorating the house.

Daddy, Momma, and me went to buy my first Christmas tree. I found the perfect one for us and I sat down right in front of it. We brought the tree home and I watched as Momma decorated the tree with pretty balls and ribbons. Luca told me these balls were special and not to be played with, or I could get into a lot of trouble.

The day came to meet Santa. When we got to the store, Luca and Abby were waiting for me. Abby is a Berner too. While waiting in line, I was so excited I could not sit still. Luca told me to be a good boy and be patient. It was hard! Finally it was our turn. Wow, I got to sit on Santa's lap! I told him I wanted a new big boy bed, toys, and treats. Santa told me to be a good boy and in a few days he would come and visit me with my presents.

Christmas morning
came and there was
my big boy bed,
cookie-man,
puppy-Santa,
and lots of
treats!

It was now late winter and my elbows started to hurt me. Momma told me that my elbows had boo-boos, but the doctor would make me feel better. The doctor said that an operation would make my boo-boos go away and I would not hurt any more.

My best friend Luca came over the night before my surgery and he brought me a big green stuffed bone toy. We ran and played with the bone for a long time. What fun we had! Luca is very thoughtful and was thinking about my feelings. Just before it was time to go, Luca and I laid down and had a talk. He told me that I would feel better after the operation and everyone at the hospital would take good care of me. He told me to take my favorite toy with me. We both decided it should be froggie. We both love froggie the most. Luca said it would make me feel like I was at home, and if I got scared I could squeeze froggie and think of him. Luca always makes me feel better. He is such a kind friend.

We got up early to get me
ready to go to the hospital.
I carried froggie with me
in the car. My tummy was
nervous, but I liked the
doctor so much, and I knew
I would feel better soon.

Everyone at the hospital was so nice to me. I remember when I woke up, the first thing I saw was froggie. I was so happy and froggie made me feel so safe. Luca was right.

After the operation I felt better. But then I got sad because the doctor said I had to rest for many weeks. I could not run or play with my best friend.

My Momma said that to pass the time we could write a book about my friendship with Luca. She also said that we could e-mail each other. My Momma has such good ideas and always makes me feel better.

Time did go by fast. It had been eight weeks since my operation and I was getting stronger each day.

The doctor said I could take short walks but could not play. I asked my Momma if we could take short walks with Luca. I was worried about Luca and missed him so much. Momma said Luca was sad and lonely. I had to see my best friend and make him happy. My Momma said yes! My little heart began to sing. I was so excited that I was going to be with my best friend! I would give him a big hug and talk to him so we would not be sad any more. This would make Luca happy, and me too!

The first time we saw each other after my operation we were so excited. We both cried happy tears. Our Moms cried too. We had missed each other so much. But we knew we would always be best friends and time would not take that away.

We go for walks around the square in town. It is such fun. We walk side by side, and talk and talk. I am so proud to be with my best friend.

We visit our friend, Abby, at her Mom's store,
and sometimes we buy new toys.

Then we have a special treat. Momma goes to the market and buys us special doggie ice cream sundaes. Wow! This is the best!

Now you know about Luca James, my best friend, my hero, and me!
Now you know about true friendship.

DEDICATIONS

To my best friend and hero, Luca James – Binkie

To my dearest husband Carl, with all my love

To my Sissy for all her love and support

To my family One and All

To my best friend Judy, whose friendship I cherish – Laura

ACKNOWLEDGMENTS

To my exceptional and most valuable team. Each of you have given your heart and soul to make my dream come true. Thank you for your devotion and continued support. Bethany Argisle, a special thanks, for always cheering me on with her never-ending advice, enthusiasm, and talent. Additional thanks for the extraordinary team brought together: Tina Davis, Albert Howell, Jessica Brunner, and Robert Bergman.

A heartfelt thanks to Jen-Ann Kirchmeier for taking my dream and bringing it to life through her watercolor illustrations.

A special thanks to Pat and Gary Leo for designing and creating the magical "Binkie Beenie."

A warm and special thank you to Janet Meadows, JC Meadows Photography, for capturing the heart and soul of Brinkley in her photographs.

ABOUT THE AUTHOR This is my first book. I do not think I would have written one if it was not for Brinkley. For years we were without a dog, thinking we would never be able to replace our dearest Springer Spaniel, Shauna Wiggles. But in September 2004, Brinkley came into our lives and changed us forever. Watching Brinkley grow has reminded me of the simplicities of life and what is truly important. He is the light of my life and my inspiration to tell his story. Brinkley, my husband Carl, and myself spend lazy dog-day afternoons living in Northern California.

ABOUT THE ILLUSTRATOR I have been an artist since childhood. I received an MFA in painting from the San Francisco Art Institute, and my art has been displayed in many exhibits throughout the country. Although I have illustrated books before, this project with Laura and Brinkley is the most exciting and alive. I live and paint in a wilderness cabin in Alaska with my fuzzy companion.